Healthy Body, Healthy Mind, Healthy Me

Living Life as the Healthiest Version of Yourself!

Elsie Edith

© Copyright 2024 - All rights reserved.

indirect, that are incurred as a result of the use of the information contained within this document, including, but not limited to, errors, omissions, or inaccuracies.

Table of Contents

Introduction

"A healthy body is formed when emotions are felt, understood, and expressed - not eaten." –Ronan Diego

Welcome to a journey like no other, a journey to the best version of you! This isn't just a book; it's a companion, a gentle guide nudging you toward a life where wellness isn't just a goal, but a joyful, everyday reality.

Have you ever stopped to ponder what "being healthy" truly means? It's easy to get lost in the whirlwind of diet trends, fitness fads, and the overwhelming sea of dos and don'ts. But here, we strip away the complexities and go back to basics. This book is your safe haven where health is not just about the absence of illness, but a harmonious blend of physical vitality, mental clarity, and a deep sense of self-worth.

Let's embark on this enlightening path together, shall we? Picture your life where each day is filled with energy, your mind is at peace, and your body is in a state of contentment. It's not a distant dream. It's a tangible, achievable reality. And the best part? The journey to get there can be as rewarding as the destination itself.

This book will challenge you, but in the best way possible. It will urge you to question the deeply ingrained beliefs you hold about health and happiness. What if I told you that being healthy isn't solely about hitting the gym or following strict diets? What if the key to true wellness lies in simple, everyday choices? In the pages that follow, you will find that health is a multifaceted gem, shining differently for each individual.

We will explore the undeniable connection between the body and the mind. The harmony between these two is crucial, yet so often overlooked. A healthy body fosters a healthy mind, and vice versa.

You'll discover that nourishing your body with the right foods, engaging in physical activity that you actually enjoy, and cultivating a positive mindset are not chores, but gifts you give yourself.

Each chapter in this book peels back a layer, revealing essential elements of a healthy life. We'll talk about nutrition, but not as you know it. Gone are the days of bland diets and unrealistic meal plans. Instead, let's celebrate food as a source of nourishment and joy. We'll redefine fitness, turning it into a fun, personalized journey rather than a one-size-fits-all regimen. And, most importantly, we'll delve into the mind, unlocking the power of positive thinking, mindfulness, and self-compassion.

As you turn these pages, you'll find stories, insights, and practical tips that are relatable, and most importantly, actionable. There's more to this than simply reading; it's about doing, feeling, and experiencing. It's about making small, sustainable changes that add up to a profound transformation. You'll learn to listen to your body, to understand its needs, and to respond with love and care.

But remember, this journey is uniquely yours. There's no competition, no rush. It's not about perfection; it's about progress and self-discovery. You'll have moments of triumph and, inevitably, moments of challenge. Embrace them all, for they are part of this beautiful journey.

Healthy Body, Healthy Mind, Healthy Me is your invitation to break free from the shackles of conventional health norms. It's a call to live life as the healthiest version of yourself, in a way that's authentic and fulfilling to you. So, take a deep breath, open your heart and mind, and let's begin this adventure together.

You're not just reading a book; you're turning a new leaf in the story of your life. A story where every chapter is more vibrant, more alive, and more "you" than ever before. Here's to the start of something wonderful: a healthier, happier, and heartier you!

Chapter 1:

Your Mindset Toward Health and

Wellness Matters

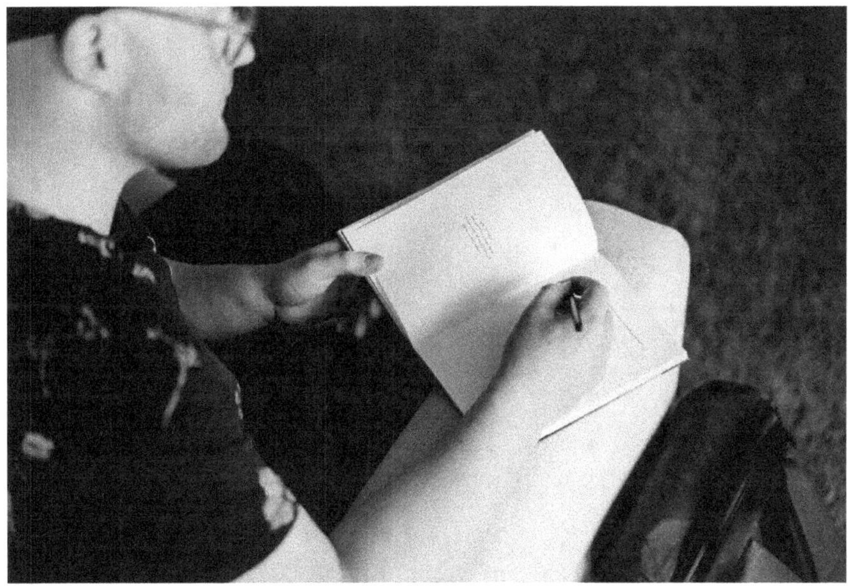

Welcome to the starting line of a race where you're guaranteed to be the winner! But wait, what race are we running? Is it the sprint to shed pounds, or the marathon to holistic health? In this chapter, we're diving deep into the world of mindsets, because what's ticking in your mind is the powerhouse driving your health journey.

Think of your mind as a garden. What seeds have you been planting? Are they seeds of fleeting diets and temporary fixes, or are they nurturing seeds of lasting health and well-being? It's time to take a magnifying glass to your subconscious thoughts. They're like the background apps on your phone—silently running, consuming energy, and shaping your everyday choices.

Let's embark on a health and fitness audit, not with a critical eye, but with a heart full of curiosity and a mind open to change. This isn't about highlighting what's "wrong" with your current lifestyle. Instead, it's about discovering the goldmine of potential that lies within you to bridge the gap between where you are and the healthiest version of yourself.

Get ready to question, explore, and perhaps rewrite your health narrative. This goes beyond losing weight; it's about gaining a life where you thrive. Let the journey begin!

Getting Clear On Your Inner Why

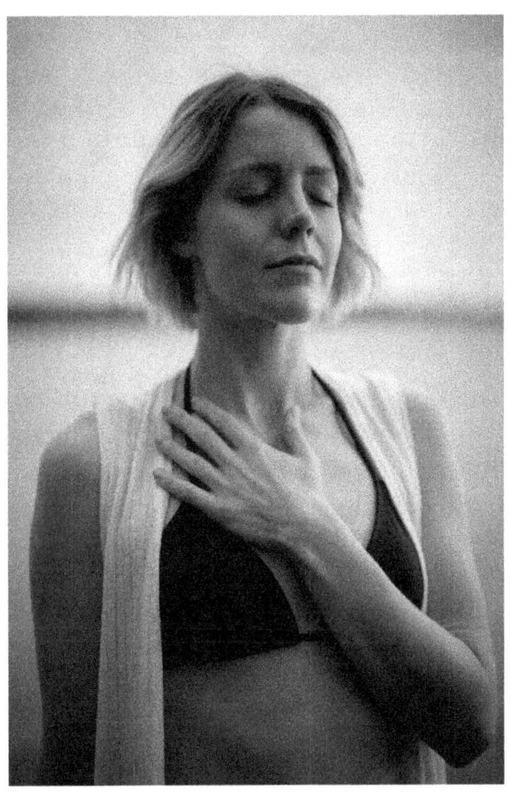

Embarking on a journey to a healthier lifestyle is like setting sail on a vast ocean. Your boat is your determination, and your compass? That's your "why." Understanding your personal motivations for seeking a healthier life is not just beneficial; it's crucial. It's the difference between wandering aimlessly and navigating with purpose.

Why is your "why" so important? It's the core essence that fuels your journey. It's about more than just losing weight or fitting into a dress size. It's about digging deeper, uncovering the genuine reasons that resonate with your core values. Maybe you're yearning for more energy to play with your kids, or perhaps you're striving for mental clarity to excel in your career. Your "why" could be as simple as wanting to wake up each day feeling good about yourself.

Understanding your "why" gives meaning to every step you take toward a healthier you. It transforms your journey from a series of tasks into a path of fulfilling personal growth. When challenges arise—

and they will—your "why" becomes your anchor, keeping you steady and focused.

So, as we set forth on this adventure, let's start by getting clear on your inner "why." It's the first step in turning your health aspirations into your lived reality.

The Power of Purpose

Harnessing the power of purpose in your health journey is akin to finding a secret superpower. When you're clear about your "why," it becomes the driving force behind every decision, action, and habit related to your health and fitness.

Firstly, purpose acts as a beacon of motivation. On days when your energy is low and your goals seem distant, remembering your "why" can reignite your drive. It's more than just shedding pounds or building muscle; it's about improving your overall health and staying energetic for your family. This intrinsic motivation is more potent and enduring than any external reward.

Additionally, a clear purpose fosters resilience. The road to health is rarely a straight path; it's fraught with obstacles and setbacks. When your actions are anchored in a meaningful "why," you're more likely to persevere through challenges. You don't just see setbacks as failures, but as opportunities to grow and reaffirm your commitment to your health.

Moreover, purpose guides your choices. With a firm understanding of your "why," you're more likely to make decisions that align with your long-term goals. It becomes easier to resist short-term temptations and stay committed to habits that serve your ultimate purpose.

Finally, purpose brings fulfillment. Achieving fitness goals is satisfying, but when these achievements are linked to a deeper purpose, they bring a sense of fulfillment that transcends physical accomplishments. You're not just working toward a healthier body, but a more fulfilled and content version of yourself.

In summary, the power of purpose in your health journey is transformative. It's not just about what you're doing; it's about why you're doing it. This purpose-driven approach leads to more consistent, meaningful, and sustainable changes in your health and fitness routines.

Self-Reflection Exercise

Ready for a little self-discovery? Grab a notebook, find a cozy spot, and let's dive into some soul-searching. This exercise is all about unearthing your true motivations for a healthier you.

Visualize Your Best Self: Close your eyes. Imagine the healthiest version of yourself. What are you doing? How do you feel? Jot down every detail.

The Joy List: Write down activities that make you genuinely happy. Do they require a certain level of health or fitness? How does being healthier enrich these joys?

Overcoming Obstacles: Think of a time you faced a health challenge. How did it make you feel? How would being healthier have changed that experience?

The Letter to Future You: Write a letter to yourself in one year. What health achievements would you like to tell yourself about? What steps did you take to get there?

The Ripple Effect: How does your health impact those around you? Consider your relationships, work, and daily interactions.

These reflections are your personal health roadmap. They're not just answers; they're the signposts guiding you toward the healthiest version of yourself. Let them light the way!

Real-Life Examples

Meet Sarah, a busy mom who found her "why" in the laughter of her kids. She wanted the energy to chase them around the park, not just watch from the sidelines. Embracing a balanced diet and fun family workouts, she's now the spirited heart of every game.

Then there's Carlos, whose "aha" moment came during a serene hike. He yearned for more of these soul-soothing adventures, realizing his fitness was key. Now, with improved stamina from regular jogging and yoga, he's scaling peaks he once only dreamed of.

Their stories echo a universal truth: when you unearth your "why," your health journey becomes not just meaningful, but a joyous adventure.

You Have a Choice to Make: What Will You Choose?

At this very moment, you stand at a crossroads. One path is worn, familiar, and easy—it's the route of old habits and comfortable routines. The other? It's less traveled, brimming with the unknown and new beginnings. This is your pivotal moment of choice: do you tread the well-worn path, or do you step boldly onto the road less traveled?

Choosing the comfort of old habits is like staying cocooned in a blanket. It's warm, it's familiar, but it also keeps you from experiencing the vibrant colors of dawn. On the other hand, embracing the challenge of new beginnings is akin to greeting the sunrise. It's fresh, it's invigorating, and it promises new light and possibilities.

This decision isn't just a single choice, but a series of choices you make every day. Each choice is a step. Do you step back into the comfort zone or stride forward toward growth and transformation?

Remember, the familiar path might seem easy, but it often leads to the same old views. The path of new beginnings, though uncertain, is where growth blossoms. It's where you discover strengths you never knew you had and joys you never thought you'd experience.

So, what will you choose? Comfort or the exhilarating journey of self-discovery and health? The roads diverge, and your story waits to be written.

Short-Term Pleasure vs. Long-Term Gain

In the quest for health, you'll often encounter two very distinct roads: the quick fix promising instant gratification and the path of sustainable health practices, a journey toward long-term well-being. It's like choosing between a sprint and a marathon. One offers immediate results with fleeting satisfaction, while the other requires patience but leads to lasting rewards.

Quick fixes are like sparklers on a summer night—they burn brightly and then fizzle out just as fast. They're the crash diets, the intense but unsustainable workout regimens, the "lose weight quick" schemes. Sure, they might give you a brief taste of satisfaction, but like a mirage, they disappear, leaving you right where you started.

On the flip side, sustainable health practices are akin to planting a garden. It requires nurturing, patience, and consistent care. You won't see the fruits of your labor immediately, but with time, your garden flourishes. These practices are your balanced diets, your enjoyable daily exercises, your mindful routines. They may not offer the instant thrill of drastic results, but their steady, enduring progress brings a sense of achievement that's both fulfilling and realistic.

Ultimately, the choice between short-term pleasure and long-term gain is about how you value your health journey. Do you seek the ephemeral glow of quick results or the enduring light of sustained well-being? Remember, true health is not a sprint; it's a lifelong marathon.

Making the Choice

Deciding to focus on your health and wellness is like making a promise to yourself. It's a journey that requires being informed, intentional, and proactive. Let's walk through how you can confidently make this choice and embark on a path to wellness that's uniquely yours.

Knowledge is Power: Start by brushing up on the basics of nutrition, the benefits of different types of exercise, and the role of mental well-being in your overall health. You don't have to dive into medical journals, but understanding these fundamentals can guide your health decisions.

Take Stock of Where You Are: It's like taking a health selfie. What's your diet like? How active are you in a typical week? How's your mental and emotional state? Knowing your current lifestyle helps in plotting a realistic course toward better health.

Goal-Setting with Precision: Instead of aiming for a nebulous target like "being healthier," set clear, attainable goals. Maybe it's incorporating a daily walk, drinking more water, or practicing mindfulness. Specific goals are stepping stones to success.

Professional Insight: Sometimes, a little expert guidance can go a long way. Chatting with a dietitian, a fitness coach, or a therapist can provide insights tailored to your personal health history and goals.

Tune Into Your Body: Your body talks, so listen to it. Recognize its cues for hunger, fatigue, or stress. Align your health choices with what your body signals to you.

Remember Your Why: Keep the reason for your health journey close to your heart. Whether it's to have more energy, reduce stress, or simply feel better day-to-day, let this "why" be the anchor that keeps you grounded in your health choices.

What Does Fitness Really Mean? It's Not What You Think

When you hear the word "fitness," what springs to mind? Is it the chiseled physique of a gym enthusiast or the endurance of a marathon runner? It's time to broaden that picture and embrace a more inclusive, holistic understanding of fitness.

Fitness, in its true essence, is not confined to the walls of a gym or the numbers on a scale. It's a multifaceted concept that encompasses physical, mental, and emotional well-being. It's about feeling strong and capable in your daily life, whether that's carrying groceries with ease, playing with your kids without getting winded, or simply walking up a flight of stairs without feeling like you've conquered Everest.

This broader perspective of fitness includes mental agility and emotional resilience. It's about having the mental stamina to tackle life's challenges and the emotional strength to maintain balance and harmony in your life.

Redefining fitness means moving away from narrow, often unattainable standards that focus solely on appearance or extreme athletic feats. It's about recognizing that fitness looks different for everyone. For some, it might be running a 5K, for others, it might be mastering a new yoga pose or simply walking more each day.

True fitness is about honoring your body's unique needs and capabilities, celebrating your progress, and embracing a lifestyle that brings joy, vitality, and balance. It's a personal journey, one where every step, no matter how small, is a step toward a healthier, happier you.

Incorporating Holistic Fitness into Daily Life

Embracing holistic fitness is about weaving wellness into the fabric of your daily life. Start by making small, manageable changes. Swap the elevator for the stairs, or try a walking meeting instead of a sit-down. Integrate stretches or simple yoga poses into your morning routine to awaken your body. Make mindfulness a daily practice, even if it's just five minutes of focused breathing or a quick meditation session. Remember, nutrition is a part of fitness too, so choose wholesome, nourishing foods that fuel your body and mind. Most importantly, listen to your body and adjust your activities to match its needs, ensuring a balanced approach to your overall well-being.

Embrace Your Journey to Holistic Health

As we close this chapter, it's important to keep in mind that your journey to health is your very own unique adventure. It's like stitching together a quilt that reflects who you are, with each piece representing the choices you make, the goals you pursue, and the little changes that bring color and texture to your life. Embracing fitness goes beyond the physical hustle; it's more about nurturing your entire being—body, mind, and spirit—in a harmonious chorus.

Hold on to the thought that every tiny step is a victory, every positive shift is meaningful, and every mindful moment enriches your overall wellness. Your path to health isn't about chasing an elusive ideal of perfection. It's an ongoing journey of discovering what fills you with energy and joy, what keeps you vibrant and thriving.

So, as you take the insights from this chapter and weave them into the fabric of your daily life, you're setting the stage for a wondrous transformation. Here's to a journey toward a healthier, happier, and more harmonious you, one step at a time. Let the beauty of your personal health journey unfold in its own time and way.

Chapter 2:

Improve Your Eating Habits and

Get Rid of Chronic Inflammation

"Every animal on Earth has its own diet; a particular way of eating that makes it possible for that animal to function at its absolute best. The same is true for human beings. There is an ideal diet for humans, but modern conveniences and food marketing campaigns have convinced us to eat in opposition to this natural way." –
Eric Edmeads

Welcome to a chapter that may very well redefine your relationship with your plate. Did you know that, according to a study, heart disease and cancer are neck-and-neck as leading causes of death, each claiming the lives of 1 in 3 people (Howard, 2019)? These aren't just alarming statistics; they're a stark reminder of how crucial our dietary choices are. Food, often hailed as our greatest medicine, is frequently ignored or mistreated, and it's time we start paying attention.

This chapter is about more than just showing exercise isn't everything for health; it also highlights how important our diet is for a good life. The truth is, while working out is important, what we eat plays a pivotal role in our overall health. Our diets can either be our greatest ally or our worst enemy.

We're also going to delve into the world of chronic inflammation—a hidden threat that is often the root cause of many health issues, including those heart-wrenching statistics we just talked about. You'll learn how the foods you choose can either contribute to or help combat this silent aggressor.

Get ready to explore how simple changes in your eating habits can have profound impacts on your health. This chapter is about transforming the way you view food—not just as a source of sustenance or pleasure, but as a powerful tool in your health toolkit. Let's embark on this journey of eating our way to better health and tackling chronic inflammation, one delicious bite at a time!

Willpower Is Neither the Problem Nor the Solution

Let's talk about willpower, that elusive force we often blame for our dietary missteps. You might think that improving your eating habits is all about boosting your willpower. Well, here's a little twist: it's not. The idea that willpower alone can overhaul your diet is as outdated as the notion that the Earth is flat. Let's debunk this myth together and explore what really influences our eating behaviors.

First up, the willpower myth. It's easy to believe that if we just had more self-control, we could easily resist that extra slice of cake or that late-night snack. But here's the thing: Willpower is like a muscle, and it gets tired. Relying solely on it to make healthy food choices is like trying to run a marathon without training. Sure, you might start strong, but soon enough, you're going to feel the burn.

Now, let's delve into the science of cravings. Cravings aren't a simple lack of self-control; they're complex responses triggered by various factors like emotions, environment, and even certain nutrient deficiencies. Ever wonder why you crave certain foods when you're stressed or tired? It's because your body is seeking a quick source of energy and comfort—and often, that comes in the form of sugary or fatty foods.

Understanding your cravings means tuning in to your body's signals. It's about recognizing the difference between physical hunger and emotional hunger. Are you really hungry, or are you bored, stressed, or sad? This understanding can shift your approach from battling cravings with willpower to addressing the underlying reasons for those cravings.

Habit Formation vs. Willpower: A Sustainable Approach to Healthy Eating

If willpower is the flash-in-the-pan, then forming habits is the slow-cooked stew of the health world. It's about building a sustainable approach to eating well, one that doesn't hinge on the whims of your self-control. Let's break down why forming habits trumps relying on willpower and how you can make this shift in a way that's as enjoyable as it is effective.

Why Habits Overpower Willpower

Willpower is like that friend who's great for a night out but can't be counted on for a long-term commitment. It's unreliable, often influenced by external factors like stress or fatigue. Habits, on the other hand, are the steadfast friends who stick around, rain or shine. They're behaviors that become automatic, requiring less mental effort and energy. When you cultivate healthy eating habits, you're programming your daily routine to include nutritious choices by default, not by force.

The Science of Habit Formation

Habits form in the brain through a process called "chunking." This is where the brain converts a sequence of actions into an automatic routine. The habit loop consists of a cue, a routine, and a reward. For example, a cue could be feeling hungry at noon, the routine is eating a healthy lunch, and the reward is feeling energized and satisfied. Identifying and understanding your habit loops is key to developing new, healthier eating patterns.

Practical Tips for Habit Change

Start Small: Begin with achievable changes. If you're not a veggie lover, start by adding one vegetable to your dinner. Small wins build momentum.

Identify Triggers: Recognize what prompts your unhealthy eating habits. Is it stress, boredom, or social settings? Once identified, you can work on healthier responses to these triggers.

Rework Your Environment: Make healthy choices easy. Keep fruits and veggies within reach and store less healthy foods out of sight.

Plan Ahead: Meal planning can be a lifesaver. Dedicate time each week to plan your meals. This reduces the likelihood of impulsive, unhealthy eating.

Associate with New Habits: Link new eating habits with existing ones. For instance, if you always have a mid-morning coffee, try pairing it with a healthy snack.

Mindful Eating: Pay attention to what you eat and savor each bite. This helps in recognizing fullness cues and enjoying your food.

Celebrate Small Victories: Acknowledge every step you take toward healthier habits. This reinforces positive behavior.

Be Patient with Yourself: Habit formation takes time. Be kind to yourself if you slip up. It's part of the journey.

Seek Social Support: Share your goals with friends or family members who can offer support and accountability.

Reflect and Tweak: Regularly assess your progress and make adjustments as needed. What works for others might not work for you, and that's okay.

Ditch the Diet Culture and Eat Healthy Instead

In a world obsessed with diet culture, it's easy to get caught up in the endless cycle of the latest diet trends. However, it's time for a reality check: Diet culture is not only often ineffective, but it can also be downright harmful. This chapter is an invitation to step off the diet roller coaster and embrace a more nourishing approach to eating.

The Downside of Diet Culture

Diet culture is like a siren song, promising quick and easy weight-loss solutions. But the truth is, it often leads to a tumultuous relationship with food, marked by cycles of restriction, guilt, and bingeing. Many diets are based on deprivation, cutting out entire food groups or drastically reducing calorie intake. This not only sets you up for nutritional imbalances but can also mess with your metabolism and mental health.

Moreover, diet culture perpetuates the harmful notion that self-worth is tied to body size, leading to a damaging mindset where food is seen as the enemy and self-esteem is constantly under siege. This mentality can lead to unhealthy eating behaviors and a disconnection from the body's natural hunger and fullness cues.

The Power of Whole Foods

Now, let's turn the page and focus on what truly works: eating whole, unprocessed foods. This isn't about a trendy diet; it's about a lifestyle change that emphasizes nourishing your body with foods that are as close to their natural state as possible.

Whole foods include a rich variety of fruits, vegetables, grains, nuts, seeds, and lean proteins. These foods are packed with essential nutrients, fiber, and antioxidants that our bodies need to function optimally. Unlike processed foods, which are often loaded with unhealthy fats, sugars, and artificial ingredients, whole foods provide sustained energy and support overall health.

Embracing whole foods means celebrating flavors and enjoying a diverse, colorful diet. It's about making peace with food and honoring your body's needs. This approach encourages mindful eating—paying attention to what, when, and how you eat. It's about listening to your body and feeding it with kindness and respect.

The beauty of whole foods is that they not only nourish your body but also your mind. A diet rich in whole foods has been linked to improved mood, better mental clarity, and a lower risk of chronic diseases.

Do You Want to Live Healthier? Try Eating Anti-Inflammatory Foods

Imagine if you could turn your meals into a health-boosting powerhouse. That's exactly what happens when you incorporate anti-inflammatory foods into your diet. Chronic inflammation is like an uninvited guest that overstays its welcome, potentially leading to various health issues. But here's the good news: your diet can be a key player in showing this guest the door.

What's the Deal with Inflammation?

Think of chronic inflammation as a low-burning flame within your body, slowly causing damage without making too much noise. This can be triggered by stress, environmental factors, and especially by what we eat. While short-term inflammation is your body's way of protecting itself, the chronic kind is the sneaky troublemaker behind many health problems.

Enter the Anti-Inflammatory Diet

The heroes of this diet are as tasty as they are beneficial. Picture vibrant leafy greens, Omega-3 rich fatty fish, wholesome grains, and an array of nuts and seeds. And let's not forget the fruits—berries and cherries are not just delicious, they're inflammation-fighting ninjas.

Spices are your secret weapon here. Turmeric, ginger, garlic, and cinnamon aren't just flavor enhancers; they're inflammation warriors. Adding these to your diet is like giving your body an extra shield against inflammation.

Making It Work for You

Integrating anti-inflammatory foods into your diet is like doing a favor for your future self. It's about simple swaps and tasty additions. Snack on almonds instead of chips, choose salmon over sausage, and drizzle olive oil instead of generic vegetable oils. Sprinkle turmeric in your curry, ginger in your tea, and a dash of cinnamon in your morning oatmeal.

It's as much about what you take away as what you include. Processed foods and sugary treats might call your name, but they're not doing your body any favors. Moderation is your friend here.

Why It's Worth It

This goes beyond dousing the flames of inflammation. It's about boosting your immune system, elevating your mood, and filling you with energy. This way of eating has its roots in longevity and vitality, and it's a celebration of food that loves you back.

So, why wait? Dive into the colorful, flavorful world of anti-inflammatory eating and watch how it transforms not just your health, but also your enjoyment of food. It's a win-win for your body and your taste buds. Let's raise a fork to healthful, delicious eating!

Chapter 3:

The Role of Mindfulness and Intentional Living in a Healthy Lifestyle

Embarking on a health journey? Brace yourself, because it's more than just what you eat and how often you exercise. Chapter 3 delves into the profound roles of mindfulness and intentional living in cultivating a truly healthy lifestyle. We're not just talking about routines and diets; we're exploring the very essence of what it means to live healthily.

Think of intentional living as your personal health GPS. It's about making conscious choices that are in sync with what you really value and want in terms of health. It's more than just going with the flow; it's about steering your life in a direction that makes you feel good, both inside and out.

And then, let's chat about mindfulness. Spoiler alert: It's not all about striking a yoga pose and chanting. Mindfulness is about soaking up the here and now, whether you're relishing a delicious meal or simply taking in the beauty of a leisurely stroll. It's about letting these mindful moments sprinkle some magic into your daily life, helping you shake off stress and embrace the healthiest version of you.

By the time you flip the last page of this chapter, you'll have a pretty neat blueprint for blending intentional living with a dash of mindfulness into a routine that's not just healthy, but also happy and whole. So, are you ready to take this exciting turn on your health journey? Let's jump in and make it an adventure to remember!

Embracing a Healthy Lifestyle Through Intentional Living

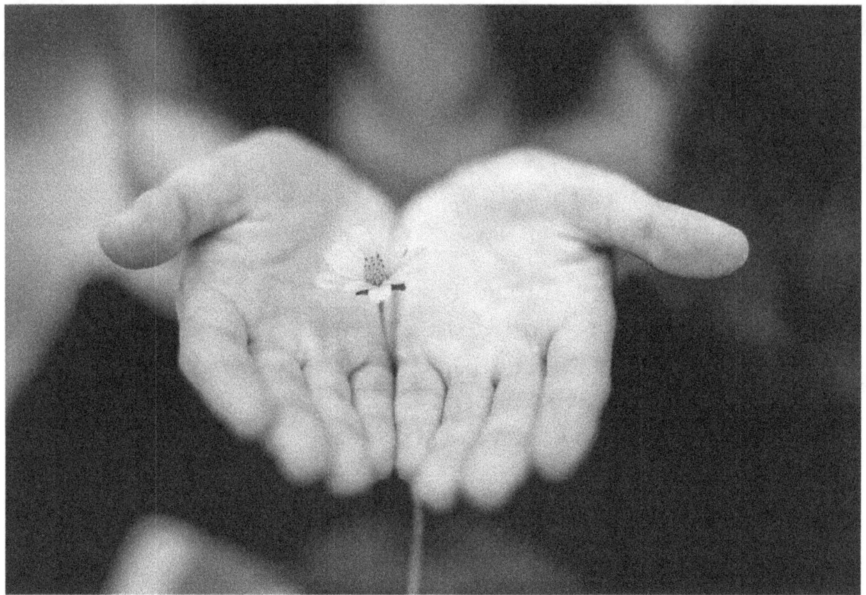

Picture this: You're at the helm of your life's ship, steering toward the shores of good health and happiness. That's intentional living for you—a journey where every choice you make is a deliberate stride toward your well-being. Intentional living isn't just a fancy term; it's a commitment to aligning your daily decisions with your deepest health and happiness goals. Let's unpack this idea and see how it can be the secret ingredient to a healthier, more joyful you.

Understanding Intentional Living

Imagine intentional living as your personal roadmap to health. It's like using a compass to navigate through life's myriad choices, ensuring you're always headed in the direction of your well-being. This approach to life is about thoughtful, purposeful decision-making. It's about living with a sense of direction and purpose, not just letting the days roll by.

The Choice is Yours

Every day, we're faced with a barrage of choices. Intentional living turns these moments into opportunities to nudge your life in the right direction. Opting for a salad over a burger, choosing a bike ride over a TV binge, or picking a good night's sleep over late-night scrolling—these aren't just random choices; they're intentional steps toward a healthier you.

Practical Intentional Living

How do you bring intentional living into your everyday life? Start simple. Define what being healthy means to you. Maybe it's feeling energized, having a clear mind, or keeping stress at bay. With this vision in mind, begin to make small, deliberate changes. Plan nutritious meals, fit in exercise you enjoy, and carve out time for relaxation. It's not about chasing perfection; it's about being a bit more mindful and deliberate with your choices.

Mindfulness: The Heart of Intentionality

Mindfulness is the secret sauce of intentional living. It means relishing your meal, feeling the air fill your lungs during a morning jog, or noticing the calm during a quiet moment. This presence deepens the connection between your actions and your health goals, making your journey more meaningful.

Intentional living can transform your health. Physically, it nurtures your body with what it needs. Mentally, it brings clarity and peace. This holistic approach is about harmonizing your physical, mental, and emotional health, creating a balanced life.

Navigating Life's Twists

Life's full of surprises, and sometimes, our plans get tossed overboard. Here's where intentional living shines. It's about adaptability—reassessing and realigning choices when life throws a curveball. It's about staying true to your course, even when the seas get rough.

Debunking The Myth: Mindfulness Is Not Meditation

Ever had one of those moments where you're completely lost in what you're doing, like savoring that first sip of coffee in the morning or getting absorbed in the colors of a sunset? That, my friends, is mindfulness in action. It's a buzzword that often gets tangled up with meditation, but let's set the record straight: mindfulness is its own wonderful beast.

What Exactly Is Mindfulness?

Mindfulness is like having a superpower where you're intensely aware of what you're feeling and sensing in the moment, without interpretation or judgment. Think of it as being the audience to your own movie, fully engaged in each scene as it unfolds.

Mindfulness vs. Meditation: The Friendly Cousins

While they're often lumped together, mindfulness and meditation are more like cousins than twins. Meditation is a more formal practice, like sitting down for a quiet session focusing on your breath or a mantra. Mindfulness, though, is the art of being fully present in the everyday hustle. It's less about finding time to sit in silence and more about finding depth in your daily doings.

Sprinkling Mindfulness into Your Day

You don't need a yoga mat or a quiet room to be mindful. It's about turning everyday activities into moments of awareness. Enjoying the texture of your food, feeling the rhythm of your walk, or simply noticing the air on your skin—that's all mindfulness. It's like turning the volume up on the little things in life.

Even in conversation, mindfulness plays a role. It's about really listening, not just waiting for your turn to speak. When you're mindful, every chat can be enriching and every interaction meaningful.

Why Mindfulness Is a Game-Changer for Health

Mindfulness isn't just good for the soul; it's a boon for the body too. By reducing stress, it can help keep your heart happy and your blood pressure in check. It sharpens your mind, clears the mental clutter, and can even bring a sense of emotional balance. For those nights when sleep plays hard to get, a dose of mindfulness can be just the ticket to dreamland.

Mindfulness also nudges you toward healthier life choices. It's about tuning in to what your body needs, whether that's nutritious food or a bit more movement. It's a mindful approach to health, taking each choice and making it count.

Living Mindfully, Intentionally, and Healthily

In the pursuit of a healthy lifestyle, two powerful allies are mindfulness and intentional living. When these two join forces, they create a synergy that not only enhances your day-to-day life but also fosters long-term health and well-being. Let's explore how to blend these concepts into a harmonious routine, navigate the inevitable challenges, and appreciate the holistic impact they have on our lives.

Combining Mindfulness and Intentional Living

Mindfulness and intentional living are like two sides of the same coin. While mindfulness teaches us to live in the present and embrace each moment, intentional living urges us to make choices that align with our deepest values and health goals. Together, they create a balanced approach to life.

Imagine you're on a hike. Mindfulness is the act of noticing the rustle of leaves, the pattern of the bark, the scent of the forest. Intentional living is choosing the path that aligns with your fitness level and interests. Both practices enhance your experience and bring a richer understanding of your journey.

Step-by-Step Guide to a Mindful, Intentional Routine

Are you game for sprinkling your day with a bit of mindfulness and thoughtful living? Here's a cozy guide to help you infuse these nuggets of joy into your everyday life. It's all about those little, meaningful rituals that can brighten up your day and bring a sense of fulfillment.

Starting with a Zen Morning: Begin each day by embracing a moment of serenity. This could be anything from taking a series of deep, grounding breaths as soon as you wake up, to relishing the aroma and taste of your morning brew, or simply sitting in quiet contemplation, setting your intentions for the day ahead.

Mindful Munching: Mealtimes are opportunities for mindfulness. Choose foods that not only tantalize your taste buds but also nourish your body. As you eat, really savor the experience: the flavors, the textures, and the feelings they evoke. Make each meal a moment of gratitude and enjoyment.

Movement with Meaning: Pick a physical activity that you genuinely enjoy and fully engage with it. It could be the gentle stretch of yoga, a lively stroll, or dancing to your favorite tunes. It's about celebrating your body's ability to move and expressing yourself through that movement.

Conscious Work and Rest: Find a balance between your work and relaxation times. Work with intention and focus, and when it's time to unwind, truly embrace the art of relaxation. Remember, resting is not time wasted; it's an essential aspect of self-care.

Reflecting at Day's End: As your day winds down, take a moment to reflect on it. Acknowledge the day's joys, the lessons learned, and consider how you'd like to grow. This evening ritual is a wonderful way to appreciate the journey of the day and set a hopeful tone for tomorrow.

These steps are more than just actions; they're the building blocks for a day filled with intention, health, and happiness. Try incorporating these practices into your daily routine and watch as they transform your ordinary days into extraordinary ones.

The Holistic Impact

When the rhythms of mindfulness and intentional living come together, it's like a melody that resonates through every aspect of your well-being. Physically, you might notice a newfound ease in managing stress, a sweet slumber at night, and a general zest for life. On the mental and emotional front, this blend can lead to clearer thinking, a focused mind, and a heart full of contentment.

But this isn't just about fleeting moments or sporadic choices; it's about weaving a tapestry of life that highlights the best of who you are. It's about crafting a way of living that not only fosters your health but also enriches every facet of your existence.

As you step onto this path, keep in mind that it's not a pursuit of flawlessness. Rather, it's about frequently choosing to be more mindful and deliberate. Every step taken, every decision made, and every moment of awareness counts, building up to a life that's richer, healthier, and more vivid.

So go ahead, let the dance of mindfulness and intentionality guide you, and watch as it turns your life into an enchanting symphony of health and joy.

Chapter 4:

What Is Intuitive Eating All About?

Step right up to Chapter 4, where we're about to embark on a delightful journey into the world of intuitive eating. Say goodbye to the tedious tallying of calories and the strict diet regimes that dampen our spirits. Intuitive eating is like having a friendly chat with your body, tuning in to its hunger signals, and eating not just with your mouth, but with your intuition.

In this chapter, we're going to peel back the layers of this refreshing approach to eating. Imagine a way of eating that's free from guilt and rules, where you get to be the expert of your own body. We'll explore how intuitive eating leads to a happier and healthier dance with your diet, one that's based on your body's natural rhythms and needs. So, get ready to learn, laugh, and maybe even let go of some old food myths as we delve into the liberating world of intuitive eating.

What Is Intuitive Eating?

In a world where diet culture often reigns supreme, intuitive eating emerges as a refreshing rebellion against the norm. It's a philosophy that turns the tables on traditional dieting, inviting you to listen to your body and eat not just with your mouth, but with your intuition. This approach promotes a healthy attitude toward food and body image, where meals become a source of nourishment and pleasure, not guilt and calculation.

Defining Intuitive Eating

Intuitive eating is like having a heartfelt conversation with your body. It's about tuning into your body's cues of hunger and fullness and responding with kindness and respect. It shifts the focus from following external dieting rules to honoring your own body's needs. This approach encourages you to trust your body to guide you in what, when, and how much to eat, fostering a harmonious relationship with food and your body.

The Psychology Behind Intuitive Eating

The essence of intuitive eating lies in its psychological underpinnings. It's based on the understanding that our bodies are naturally wired to send signals of hunger and fullness. By paying attention to these cues, you can maintain a balanced diet that's right for your body. This practice also involves recognizing and respecting your body's natural diversity, understanding that healthy bodies come in all shapes and sizes.

Intuitive eating challenges the common notion that you need to control or suppress your hunger to achieve a certain body type. Instead, it encourages you to embrace your body's natural instincts, which are often smarter than any diet plan out there.

Contrast with Traditional Dieting

Traditional dieting is like following a strict recipe—it often involves rigid rules, calorie counting, and a focus on weight loss. Diets are typically built on the premise of external control and deprivation, which can lead to a cycle of yo-yo dieting, guilt, and body dissatisfaction.

Intuitive eating, on the other hand, is like freestyle cooking. It rejects the diet mentality of "good" and "bad" foods, calorie counting, and restrictive eating. This approach advocates for a more natural, individualized way of eating that honors your body's hunger, recognizes fullness, and finds satisfaction in eating.

While traditional diets often lead to short-term weight loss followed by regain (and often additional weight), intuitive eating aims for long-term health and well-being. It's not a diet but a lifestyle—one that promotes a sustainable, positive relationship with food.

Benefits of Intuitive Eating

The benefits of intuitive eating extend far beyond just physical health. It fosters a positive body image and a healthy mind. It encourages you to break free from the cycle of chronic dieting and the emotional turmoil that often comes with it. By learning to trust your body and its hunger signals, you cultivate a sense of freedom and empowerment in your eating habits.

Moreover, intuitive eating aligns with mindful eating practices. It encourages you to be present with your food, to savor each bite, and to enjoy the experience of eating. This mindfulness can lead to better digestion, greater satisfaction with meals, and a healthier approach to food in general.

The 10 Principles of Intuitive Eating

Embarking on the intuitive eating journey is like setting out on a path to rediscover and reconnect with your body's natural instincts around food. This approach is built on 10 foundational principles that collectively guide you toward a healthier, more peaceful relationship with food and your body.

Reject the Diet Mentality

This principle calls for a full break-up with diets. It's about letting go of the false hope of quick weight loss and the cycle of guilt that often comes with dieting. Rejecting the diet mentality means opening your mind to a new way of thinking about food—one that isn't dictated by restrictive eating patterns.

Honor Your Hunger

Keeping your body biologically fed with adequate energy and carbohydrates is key to honoring your hunger. Listen for the early signs of hunger and feed your body respectfully. Ignoring these signals can trigger a primal drive to overeat, and usually, the foods you end up consuming are the ones you've been trying to avoid.

Make Peace with Food

Give yourself unconditional permission to eat. When you tell yourself you can't or shouldn't have a particular food, it can lead to feelings of deprivation, which often culminate in binge eating. By allowing all foods, you eliminate the power and emotion they may hold over you.

Challenge the Food Police

The food police are the voices in your head that declare you as "good" for eating minimal calories or "bad" because you ate a piece of chocolate cake. Challenging these thoughts is crucial in intuitive eating, as it allows you to break free from the guilt and shame often associated with eating.

Discover the Satisfaction Factor

In our rush to comply with diet culture, we often overlook one of the most basic gifts of existence: the pleasure and satisfaction that can be found in the eating experience. When you eat what you really want, in an environment that is inviting, the pleasure you derive will be a powerful guide in helping you decide when you have had enough.

Feel Your Fullness

Listen for the body signals that tell you that you are no longer hungry. Observe the signs that show that you're comfortably full. Pause in the middle of eating and ask yourself how the food tastes, and what your current hunger level is.

Cope with Your Emotions with Kindness

First, recognize that food restriction, both physically and mentally, can, in itself, trigger loss of control, which can feel like emotional eating. Find kind ways to comfort, nurture, distract, and resolve your issues without using food. Anxiety, loneliness, boredom, and anger are emotions we all experience throughout life; food won't fix any of these feelings.

Respect Your Body

Accept your genetic blueprint. Just as a person with a shoe size of eight would not expect to realistically squeeze into a size six, it is equally futile (and uncomfortable) to have a similar expectation about body size. Respect your body, so you can feel better about who you are.

Movement - Feel the Difference

Forget militant exercise. Just get active and feel the difference. Shift your focus to how it feels to move your body, rather than the calorie-burning effect of exercise. If you focus on how you feel from working out, such as energized, it can make the difference between rolling out of bed for a brisk morning walk or hitting the snooze alarm.

Honor Your Health with Gentle Nutrition

Make food choices that honor your health and taste buds while making you feel good. Remember that you don't have to eat a perfect diet to be healthy. It's what you eat consistently over time that matters. Progress, not perfection, is what counts.

Each of these principles plays a vital role in guiding you toward a more intuitive, mindful approach to eating. Together, they pave the way for a healthier relationship with food, where eating becomes a source of nourishment and joy, not anxiety and control.

Embarking on the Ayurveda Adventure

Welcome to the colorful and aromatic world of Ayurveda, where every meal is an opportunity to nourish not just the body but also the soul. Originating from an ancient Indian philosophy, this approach to eating is like a dance with nature, where food is both a delight and a healer. Let's take a walk through this vibrant landscape and discover how Ayurveda principles can add a sprinkle of wisdom to your eating habits.

Discovering Your Dosha

Ayurveda introduces us to the concept of doshas: Vata, Pitta, and Kapha. Think of them as your personal health guides, each with its unique set of characteristics.

Vata (Air and Space): The creative and lively bunch. They're at their best with nourishing, grounding meals that bring warmth and stability.

Pitta (Fire and Water): The fiery go-getters. They thrive on cooling and calming foods that keep their inner flames balanced.

Kapha (Earth and Water): The calm and loving souls. Energizing foods that spark their vitality are their best friends.

Knowing your dosha is like having a secret map to the foods that make you feel fantastic.

The Ayurveda Palate

Ayurveda is a kaleidoscope of flavors and principles:

Eating for Your Dosha

In Ayurveda, eating for your dosha means selecting foods that bring balance and harmony to your unique constitution. Each dosha—Vata, Pitta, and Kapha—has specific dietary recommendations:

- **Vata:** Being airy and light, Vata types benefit from warm, grounding, and moist foods. Think cooked grains, hearty soups, and nuts. Spices like ginger and cumin can also be soothing.

- **Pitta:** With their fiery nature, Pittas thrive on cooling foods. Fresh fruits, vegetables, and dairy products can help balance their inner heat. Spices like coriander and fennel are beneficial, while hot spices should be minimized.

- **Kapha:** Kaphas do well with light, dry, and warm foods to counterbalance their earthy and moist nature. Think grilled lean meats, leafy greens, and a variety of legumes. Spicy foods like chili can stimulate a Kapha's metabolism.

The Six Tastes

Ayurveda identifies six tastes (Shad Rasa) that are important for a balanced diet:

- **Sweet:** Nourishing and building, including grains, fruits, and natural sweeteners.

- **Sour:** Stimulating and energizing, like citrus fruits and fermented foods.

- **Salty:** Maintaining the body's electrolyte balance, found in salt and seaweed.

- **Bitter:** Detoxifying and light, including leafy greens and herbs.

- **Pungent:** Heating and metabolizing, found in spicy foods and certain vegetables like onions.

- **Astringent:** Cooling and anti-inflammatory, such as legumes and raw fruits.

Including all six tastes in each meal ensures a well-rounded diet, offering a spectrum of nutrients and keeping cravings in check.

Mindful Combos and Timing

Ayurveda emphasizes not just what you eat but how and when you eat:

- **Combining Foods Mindfully:** Ayurveda suggests avoiding incompatible food combinations (like fruit with meals) that can disturb digestion. Instead, it encourages combining foods that complement each other and enhance digestion.

- **Eating in Sync with Natural Rhythms:** Aligning mealtimes with your body's natural rhythms maximizes digestion and energy. A hearty breakfast and lunch with a lighter dinner, ideally before sunset, are recommended.

- **Mindful Eating Practices:** Eating in a calm and relaxed environment, chewing food thoroughly, and being present during meals enhance the digestive process and the overall eating experience.

Merging Ayurveda with Intuitive Eating

Now, let's blend the ancient wisdom of Ayurveda with the modern savvy of intuitive eating. Imagine using Ayurveda's insights to understand your body's needs, then applying intuitive eating to listen and respond to your body's hunger and fullness signals. It's a dynamic duo that brings together the best of structure and flexibility.

- **Listen and Learn:** Ayurveda gives you the "why," and intuitive eating focuses on the "how" of eating.

- **Flexibility in Balance:** While Ayurveda might nudge you toward certain foods, intuitive eating reminds you to enjoy your meals without guilt.

- **Savor the Moment:** Both paths champion the art of eating mindfully—relishing every bite with joy and presence.

- **A Holistic Approach:** Embrace other Ayurveda practices like yoga to support your journey toward a blissful balance of mind, body, and spirit.

What Kind of Exercise Is The Right One For You?

Welcome to Chapter 5, where we're about to debunk a major fitness myth! If you've ever felt the pressure of fitting into the one-size-fits-all exercise mold, you're in for a refreshing revelation. This chapter is all about understanding that the best workout routine is as unique as you are. Just like our fingerprints, our bodies and their needs are distinct. So, it's time to toss out the notion that everyone needs to grind for hours at the gym to be considered fit.

Get ready to explore a world of fitness that celebrates diversity, honors individuality, and focuses on what truly works for you. From yoga enthusiasts to trail runners, from dance lovers to strength training aficionados, everyone has their own perfect fit when it comes to exercise. Let's embark on this journey to discover yours!

What Is Holistic Health and Why Does It Matter?

Imagine your health as a beautiful, lush garden. Just as a garden thrives with the right balance of sunlight, water, and care, your well-being flourishes when you nurture all aspects of yourself—body, mind, and spirit. This is the essence of holistic health: a vibrant, all-encompassing approach to living that weaves together the physical, mental, and emotional strands of life into a harmonious tapestry.

Defining Holistic Health

Holistic health is like being the conductor of your own personal orchestra. Each section—whether it's the strings of your physical health, the woodwinds of your mental state, or the brass of your emotional well-being—needs to be in tune and balanced. It's about looking at yourself as a whole, understanding that a pain in the body might be linked to stress in the mind or turbulence in the emotions.

The Magic of a Holistic Approach

Embracing a holistic approach is like putting on a pair of 3D glasses. Suddenly, you see the depth and interconnectedness of your health. It's about recognizing that true wellness transcends having a toned body or a diet free of junk food; it's also about nurturing a positive mindset, managing stress, and allowing emotional expression. This approach doesn't just patch up problems; it nurtures lasting, sustainable well-being.

The Perks of Holistic Practices

Diving into holistic practices is like exploring a treasure chest of well-being. These practices come with a bouquet of benefits:

For the Body: From yoga's graceful stretches to Tai Chi's flowing movements, holistic physical practices keep your body supple, energized, and strong. Eating wholesome, natural foods ensures your body gets the best fuel to thrive.

For the Mind: Meditation, mindfulness, and even simple breathing exercises sharpen your focus, clear mental fog, and boost brainpower. They're like a spa day for your mind, leaving you refreshed and rejuvenated.

For the Emotions: Holistic health values your emotional landscape. Techniques like journaling or engaging in creative arts provide outlets for expression, helping to maintain an emotional equilibrium.

The Ripple Effect: The beauty of a holistic approach is that it creates a ripple effect. A brisk walk (physical) can lift your spirits (emotional) and clear your mind (mental). Likewise, a few minutes of meditation (mental) can ease bodily tension (physical) and bring emotional peace.

What Kind of Exercise Does Your Body Need?

Embarking on a fitness journey can sometimes feel like trying to find the perfect pair of jeans—it's all about finding what fits you best. Just as we all have unique personalities, our bodies have their own preferences and needs when it comes to exercise. Let's navigate the fitness landscape to discover what kind of exercise resonates with your body.

Understanding Your Body

Your body communicates with you, albeit not in words. Listening to it is like learning a new language, one where aches and energy levels are the vocabulary. To understand what exercise your body needs, tune into how different activities make you feel. Do you feel invigorated after a run, or do you prefer the muscle-strengthening buzz from lifting weights? Observing how your body and mood respond to different types of physical activity can be a revealing guide.

Cardio vs. Strength Training

The cardio vs. strength training debate is like choosing between coffee and tea—both are great, but you might have a preference. Cardio exercises, like running, swimming, or cycling, are fantastic for heart health and endurance. Strength training, on the other hand, builds muscle, boosts metabolism, and strengthens bones.

Your choice might depend on your goals. Looking to shed some pounds or improve endurance? Cardio might be your best friend. Want to tone up or gain muscle strength? Say hello to weights. The best part? You don't have to pick sides. A balanced routine often includes a mix of both.

Beyond Traditional Workouts

The fitness world is a vast ocean with more than just the islands of cardio and strength training. Yoga, Qigong, and Tai Chi are like hidden gems beneath the surface. These practices not only enhance physical fitness but also bring a sense of calm and balance. They're fantastic for flexibility, core strength, and mental tranquility. Plus, they're a great fit for those seeking a gentler approach to fitness.

Customizing Your Exercise Plan

Crafting your exercise plan is like painting: You have a palette of options to create something that's uniquely yours. Start by defining your fitness goals. Are you aiming for flexibility, muscle tone, cardiovascular health, or stress reduction? Then, consider your lifestyle. Do you prefer gym workouts, outdoor activities, or home-based exercises?

Mix and match different types of exercises to keep your routine interesting and comprehensive. Remember, consistency is key, so choose activities you enjoy. Love dancing? Incorporate Zumba or salsa classes. Prefer the great outdoors? Hiking or cycling might be up your alley.

Interactive Activity: Designing Your Own Health and Fitness Action Plan Including Mindset and Routine Transformation

Creating a personal health and fitness action plan is like crafting your very own roadmap to wellness. It's about setting goals, incorporating holistic practices, and establishing a routine that aligns with your lifestyle. Let's jump into this interactive activity to transform your health and fitness mindset and routine.

Setting Personal Goals

- **Define Your Vision:** Start by envisioning your ideal state of health and fitness. What does it look like and feel like?

- **Set SMART Goals:** Make your goals Specific, Measurable, Achievable, Relevant, and Time-bound.

- **Create Mini-Goals:** Break down your larger goals into smaller, manageable steps. This could be as simple as adding one more fruit to your diet daily or taking a 10-minute walk every morning.

Incorporating Holistic Practices into Daily Life

- **Yoga:** Begin or end your day with yoga to enhance physical flexibility, build strength, and foster mental relaxation. Choose a style that resonates with your current fitness level and goals.

- **Meditation and Micro-Meditations:** Dedicate a few minutes each day for meditation. Micro-meditations can be done anywhere—even during a coffee break—to clear your mind and reduce stress.

- **Mindfulness Activities:** Implement mindfulness practices such as Awe Walks, where you observe and appreciate your surroundings, or Body Scan Meditations, focusing on each part of your body to release tension.

- **Healthy Coping Mechanisms:** Develop strategies to manage anxiety and stress, like deep breathing exercises, journaling, or engaging in a hobby that calms your mind.

Creating a Balanced Routine

- **Daily or Weekly Planner:** Use a planner to schedule your activities. Balance your routine with a mix of exercise, relaxation, and mindfulness practices.

- **Variety is Key:** Include different types of activities to keep your routine interesting and cover all aspects of wellness—cardio, strength training, flexibility, and relaxation.

- **Regular Check-ins:** Set aside time each week to reflect on your progress and make adjustments as needed.

Rethinking Workout Duration

- **Quality Over Quantity:** Understand that a one-hour workout isn't a magic formula for everyone. Focus on the quality and intensity of your workouts rather than just duration.

- **Short and Effective Workouts:** Explore high-intensity interval training (HIIT) or circuit training, which can be effective in shorter durations.

- **Integrate Movement into Your Day:** Find ways to be more active throughout your day—take the stairs, stretch during work breaks, or have a dance break.

Designing your own health and fitness action plan is a fun and empowering process. It's about listening to your body, being mindful of your needs, and creating a routine that brings joy and vitality. Remember, this plan is a living document—it can evolve as you grow and change. The key is to stay committed, be flexible, and enjoy the journey to a healthier, happier you.

Your Path to Wellness: A Personalized and Holistic Approach

And here we are, at the end of a delightful stroll through the garden of health and wellness. If there's one golden nugget to take away, it's this: Your health journey is as unique as your favorite playlist. Embracing personalized health isn't just a trend; it's about tuning into the rhythm of your own body and mind and finding what makes you feel like the best version of yourself.

Think of your wellness journey as a custom-made outfit, tailored just for you. Whether it's the energizing buzz of a spin class, the zen of a sunrise yoga session, or the serene focus of a meditation practice, each element of your routine should fit you perfectly. Your fitness and wellness choices should be like your favorite clothes: comfortable, suited to your style, and making you feel fabulous.

Remember, the path to holistic wellness is an ever-evolving road. It's okay to try new things, to change your routine, and to adapt as your life changes. The beauty of this journey lies in its flexibility and the joy of discovering what works for you at different stages of your life.

Conclusion

As we turn the final page of this enlightening journey through *Healthy Body, Healthy Mind, Healthy Me*, it's clear that the adventure toward the healthiest version of yourself is just beginning. This book has been more than a collection of chapters; it's a toolkit, a companion, and a source of inspiration for your journey to holistic wellness.

We've delved into the power of mindset, the wisdom of intuitive eating, the personalization of exercise, and the harmony of holistic health practices. Each chapter has aimed to light a spark within you—to ignite a passion for a lifestyle that is as fulfilling and joyful as it is healthy and sustainable.

Remember, your journey to health is deeply personal and uniquely yours. It's not a race, nor is it a competition. It's about finding what works for you, embracing changes, and celebrating each small victory along the way. This journey is about growth, learning, and self-discovery. It's about listening to your body, understanding your needs, and nurturing your well-being at every level.

As you move forward, carry with you the lessons and insights from this book. Let them guide you, inspire you, and remind you that being healthy is about more than just physical fitness; it's about a balanced, joyful, and enriched life.

So, here's to you and your journey to health. May it be a path filled with discovery, joy, and an abundance of wellness. Remember, the journey may conclude in these pages, but your adventure toward a healthier, happier, and heartier you continues. Here's to embracing your healthiest self—every step of the way!

References

Amy. (2018, November 8). *Intuitive Eating Principle One {Reject the Diet Mentality}*. Love Your Body Well. https://loveyourbodywell.net/intuitive-eating-principle-1/

ayurveda for beginners. (2021, July 30). Loose Leaf Soul - the Holistic Lifestyle Blog. https://www.looseleafsoul.com/blog-1/ayurveda-a-crash-course

Bannis, S. (2018, May 31). *7 Tips for Transitioning Into a Healthier Lifestyle*. City of Creative Dreams. https://www.cityofcreativedreams.com/7-tips-for-transitioning-into-a-healthier-lifestyle/

Blake-Richards, A. (2021, March 30). *Are You Eating the Right Way?* WILDFIT®. https://getwildfit.com/are-you-eating-the-right-way/

Conscious Lifestyle. (2017a, January 8). *The 7 Commandments of Health: What the World's Healthiest Diets Have in Common*. Conscious Lifestyle Magazine. https://www.consciouslifestylemag.com/healthiest-diet-foods-eating/

Conscious Lifestyle. (2017b, February 9). *The Art of Mindful Eating: Simple Practices for Greater Health & Happiness*. Conscious Lifestyle Magazine. https://www.consciouslifestylemag.com/mindful-eating-food-health/

Harvard Health Publishing. (2023, April 15). *Quick-start guide to an anti‑inflammation diet*. Harvard Health. https://www.health.harvard.edu/staying-healthy/quick-start-guide-to-an-antiinflammation-diet

Howard, J. (2019, September 3). Cancer now tops heart disease as the No. 1 cause of death in these countries. CNN. https://edition.cnn.com/2019/09/03/health/leading-cause-of-death-cancer-heart-disease-study/index.html

Lailah. (2019, December 8). *11 Healthy Habits To Start A Holistic Lifestyle*. Daily Diet Dish. https://www.dailydietdish.com/start-a-holistic-lifestyle/

MacMillan, A. (2023). *What Is Intuitive Eating? A Nutritionist Weighs In On This Popular Anti-Diet.* Health. https://www.health.com/nutrition/intuitive-eating

Mehdi, S. (2015, April 3). *30-Minute Yoga Routine For A Healthy You.* STYLECRAZE. https://www.stylecraze.com/articles/minute-yoga-routine-for-a-healthy-you/

Mischke, M. (2024). *How to Improve Digestion.* Www.banyanbotanicals.com. https://www.banyanbotanicals.com/info/ayurvedic-living/living-ayurveda/health-guides/understanding-agni

Mylene Rietkerk. (2021, June 2). *THE RELATIONSHIP BETWEEN FOOD AND YOUR MENTAL AND EMOTIONAL HEALTH.* Mylene RIETKERK. https://mylenerietkerk.com/the-relationship-between-food-and-your-mental-and-emotional-health/

Rachel, A. (2019). *Everything You Need to Know About Holistic Living + 8 Ways to Live a Holistic Lifestyle – Ashley Rachel Coaching.* Lovely Holistic Living. https://www.lovelyholisticliving.com/ways-to-embrace-holistic-living-for-beginners/

Rebecca. (2020, December 6). *What is Ayurveda? A Beginners Guide.* Ayurveda with Rebecca. https://ayurvedawithrebecca.com/what-is-ayurveda-a-beginners-guide/

Sauchelli, S. (2023, February 13). *How to Eat Healthy Without Going on a Diet: Ultimate Guide.* Thriving & Inspiring.

https://www.thrivingandinspiring.com/how-to-eat-healthy-without-going-on-a-diet/

Spritzler, F. (2018). *Anti-Inflammatory Diet 101: How to Reduce Inflammation Naturally*. Healthline. https://www.healthline.com/nutrition/anti-inflammatory-diet-101

The WILDFIT Team. (2020, December 8). *8 Reasons Why Diets Fail*. WILDFIT®. https://getwildfit.com/8-reasons-why-diets-fail/

What does "Getting Fit", actually mean? - Personal Best Fitness. (n.d.). Personal Best Fitness. https://www.personalbestfitness.com.au/what-does-getting-fit-actually-mean/

Zweig, K. (2022, August 23). What Does It Mean to Be Healthy? *Psychology Today*. https://www.psychologytoday.com/intl/blog/ounce-prevention-md/202208/what-does-it-mean-be-healthy

Image References

Bashar, D. (2018). Mujer con chaleco blanco y bikini negro con la mano en el pecho. In *Unsplash*. https://unsplash.com/es/fotos/mujer-con-chaleco-blanco-y-bikini-negro-con-la-mano-en-el-pecho-xMNel_otvWs

Brown, J. (2020). Mujer con camiseta sin mangas negra y pantalones negros sentada en el suelo sosteniendo una taza de cerámica azul durante. In *Unsplash*. https://unsplash.com/es/fotos/mujer-con-camiseta-sin-mangas-negra-y-pantalones-negros-sentada-en-el-suelo-sosteniendo-una-taza-de-ceramica-azul-durante-BCFLDSZ-og8

Caesar, J. (2015). Foto de mujer en campo de hierba verde al aire libre durante el día. In *Unsplash*.

https://unsplash.com/es/fotos/foto-de-mujer-en-campo-de-hierba-verde-al-aire-libre-durante-el-dia-DYTQrnJ5FJ0

Desai, B. (2019). Planta de hoja verde. In *Unsplash.* https://unsplash.com/es/fotos/planta-de-hoja-verde-8N1eixz3M7c

Finde Zukunft. (2021). Hombre en camiseta negra sosteniendo papel blanco de impresora. In *Unsplash.* https://unsplash.com/es/fotos/hombre-en-camiseta-negra-sosteniendo-papel-blanco-de-impresora-0gj1gfvm008

Florin, R. (2018). Mujer con camiseta blanca de cuello redondo sosteniendo su cabeza. In *Unsplash.* https://unsplash.com/es/fotos/mujer-con-camiseta-blanca-de-cuello-redondo-sosteniendo-su-cabeza-CwTBt6jyagQ

Grabwowska, M. (2019). Ensalada de verduras. In *Unsplash.* https://unsplash.com/es/fotos/ensalada-de-verduras-pCxJvSeSB5A

Hisel, A. (2021). Mujer con sujetador deportivo rojo y leggings morados. In *Unsplash.* https://unsplash.com/es/fotos/mujer-con-sujetador-deportivo-rojo-y-leggings-morados-Nqeyae9jOd4

Kleinheider, L. (2017). Un hombre con gafas mirando por una ventana. In *Unsplash.* https://unsplash.com/es/fotos/un-hombre-con-gafas-mirando-por-una-ventana-OsC8HauR0e0

Lark, B. (2017a). Cerezas negras y rojas en cuenco blanco. In *Unsplash.* https://unsplash.com/es/fotos/cerezas-negras-y-rojas-en-cuenco-blanco-nTZOILVZuOg

Lark, B. (2017b). Huevo escalfado con verduras y tomates en plato azul. In *Unsplash.* https://unsplash.com/es/fotos/huevo-escalfado-con-verduras-y-tomates-en-plato-azul-jUPOXXRNdcA

Lark, B. (2017c). Plato de cerámica blanca junto a cuchara de acero gris. In *Unsplash*. https://unsplash.com/es/fotos/plato-de-ceramica-blanca-junto-a-cuchara-de-acero-gris-nBtmglfY0HU

Merchán Montes, P. (2018). Mujer sosteniendo tenedor en la mesa delantera. In *Unsplash*. https://unsplash.com/es/fotos/mujer-sosteniendo-tenedor-en-la-mesa-delantera-Orz90t6o0e4

Price, M. (2017). Dos mujeres y dos niños en brazos mientras estaban sentados fuera de casa. In *Unsplash*. https://unsplash.com/es/fotos/dos-mujeres-y-dos-ninos-en-brazos-mientras-estaban-sentados-fuera-de-casa-kvHP-ueoMNI

Shani, M. (2020). Plato de pasta en cuenco de cerámica negra. In *Unsplash*. https://unsplash.com/es/fotos/plato-de-pasta-en-cuenco-de-ceramica-negra-X8E69TKb52k

Shaw, C. (2020). Mujer en vestido blanco sosteniendo taza de cerámica blanca. In *Unsplash*. https://unsplash.com/es/fotos/mujer-en-vestido-blanco-sosteniendo-taza-de-ceramica-blanca-i1zD8-hp9xg

Street, J. (2016). Cuenco en forma de corazón con fresas. In *Unsplash*. https://unsplash.com/es/fotos/cuenco-en-forma-de-corazon-con-fresas-tb5A-QTI6xg

Trochez, L. (2017). Fotografía de enfoque selectivo de mujer sosteniendo flores de pétalos amarillos. In *Unsplash*. https://unsplash.com/es/fotos/fotografia-de-enfoque-selectivo-de-mujer-sosteniendo-flores-de-petalos-amarillos-ktPKyUs3Qjs

Vega, K. (2018). Fotografía de silueta de mujer haciendo yoga. In *Unsplash*. https://unsplash.com/es/fotos/fotografia-de-silueta-de-mujer-haciendo-yoga-F2qh3yjz6Jk

Winegart, K. (2020). Hombre con camiseta negra y pantalones cortos blancos caminando sobre piso de madera marrón. In *Unsplash*. https://unsplash.com/es/fotos/hombre-con-camiseta-negra-y-pantalones-cortos-blancos-caminando-sobre-piso-de-madera-marron-eGSBVVtVCCw